WHAT A HOPE!

by

Gilbert Ellis

Salvation Books
The Salvation Army International Headquarters
London, United Kingdom

First published 2010
© 2010
The General of The Salvation Army

ISBN 978-0-85412-817-4

Cover design and artwork by Nathan Sigauke

Published by Salvation Books
The Salvation Army International Headquarters
101 Queen Victoria Street, London EC4V 4EH, United Kingdom

Printed by UK Territory Print & Design Unit

In grateful memory of Colonel Rhys Dumbleton,
who enthusiastically read and discussed the subject of this
book until hope was changed to sight at the age of 93.

Abbreviations

GNB   Good News Bible (Today's English Version), © 1976 American
Bible Society, New York

KJV   King James (Authorised) Version

NKJV New King James Version, © 1982 by Thomas Nelson, Inc.

NLT   New Living Translation, © Tyndale House Publishers, 1996, 1998

SASB The Song Book of The Salvation Army, 1986 edition

Contents

Introduction

BREATHING – it's an activity we maintain from the moment we are born until the instant we die. We seldom think about it. It's automatic, and we do not give it our attention unless it becomes a problem. It's much the same with hope. We just accept it as part of our Christian life and don't think much about it unless there's a problem. Yet the two – breathing and hope – are related. The word 'aspire' is related to both breath and hope. Both are God-given. When we stop breathing or hoping, we also stop living.

What's so special about hope? When it comes to our spiritual life Paul tells us there are three elements that should constantly be present. At the conclusion of the 13th chapter of his First Letter to the Corinthians, Paul writes that as life matured he put aside many of the childish things in his life that were no longer important for him. He concluded that three things remain: faith, hope and love. He went on to add, 'The greatest of these is love.' It is interesting to note that he describes these elements as things that remain or abide, that is to say, they are constant in his life. They were always present in Paul's life, and we need them in our lives too.

The whole of chapter 13 is devoted to the concept of love, which he rightly says is the greatest of the three. This 'Love Chapter', as it is often called, is one of the most important and well known portions of the Bible. Books without number have been written on the subject of love, but this chapter is sublime.

The first 'constant element' which Paul mentions is faith. As a central and essential quality for everyone who would know God, it is mentioned in John 3:16 as the response we need to make to the revealed Love of God. Like love it has a chapter dedicated to it – the 'Faith Chapter' is Hebrews 11.

But the second quality of the three mentioned by Paul has not received the same amount of attention. It is included with the other two in John 3:16, but not directly by name. Just reflect for a moment on this verse as it is recorded in the *Contemporary English Version*: 'God loved the people of this world so much that he gave his only Son, so that everyone who has faith in him will have eternal life and never really die.'

Love is mentioned, as is faith, but hope is implied in the last part of the verse. We could paraphrase this verse as follows: 'God loves us, and if we put our faith in him we have hope.' Love and faith are mentioned in John 3:16, but hope is implied. Love and faith have their special descriptive chapters, but hope has no such chapter, yet it is present in both the other chapters. Hope is linked with faith and love in 1 Corinthians 13:13, and hope is included in Hebrews 11. For example in verse 16: 'they were longing for a better country – a heavenly one.' Also in the closing two verses, 39–40: 'These were all commended for their faith, and none of them received what had been promised. God had planned something better for us so that only together with us would they be made perfect.'

If John is the apostle of love, and Peter the apostle of faith, then surely Paul is the apostle of hope. As you read the pages of this book, you will see that it is Paul who puts hope in the limelight. Most of the Scripture references to the subject and nature of hope are attributable to Paul. Although hope is a thread that can be found throughout the Bible, it is Paul who expands its meaning and importance for the Christian.

While faith and love are more directly mentioned and demonstrated, hope is usually just implied, often hidden beneath the surface. This I believe is also reflected in the writings and sermons that are written and preached today. It is no longer fashionable to mention it.

In the early days of The Salvation Army the Movement was inspired by hope. The first Salvationists truly believed they were going to win the world for God. Their warlike songs reflected this and they wrote it on their banners. It was this hope that created enthusiasm which knew no bounds. The other hope that inspired them was the hope of Heaven. Because death was a constant companion it was sung and preached about much more. Life was insecure, and death could strike down anyone at any time; children, adults in their prime – not just the elderly. When I went to Sunday school a favourite song of the time was, 'There's a home for little children above the bright blue sky'. It was written when child deaths were not uncommon. Not surprisingly, this song is rarely sung today.

Early-day Salvationists used to sing songs like: 'Are you ready to die?' and 'One sweetly solemn thought comes to me o'er and o'er. I'm nearer home today, today, than ever I've been before!' These songs are no longer in The Salvation Army's songbook, although the tune 'Nearer Home' is! One song that is still in the songbook, and which was used frequently in the pioneer days of The Salvation Army especially when it opened up in a new country is:

> We're bound for the land of the pure and the holy,
> The home of the happy, the Kingdom of love;
> Ye wanderers from God in the broad road of folly,
> O say, will you go to the Eden above?
>
> Will you go? Will you go?
> O say, will you go to the Eden above?

(William Hunter *SASB* 905)

Somehow the question, 'Where will you spend eternity?' no longer seems relevant. People are living for the present, with little or no thought for tomorrow. The story is told of someone waiting at a bus shelter where a poster was on display posing the question, 'Where will you be on the day of judgment?' In understandable frustration, the person wrote on the poster, 'Still waiting here for the 211 bus.'

Death has been banished from the public arena, and with it much of the need for hope. Hope has become equated with 'Pie in the sky when you die', and is therefore reduced to wishful or escapist thinking. So while the subjects of love and faith are presented and discussed at great length, hope is given just lip service, a side issue, mentioned as a passing thought, briefly referred to, but seldom developed.

Yet the Bible is permeated with hope.

In the first book of the Bible, during the expulsion of Adam and Eve from the Garden of Eden, we read of a curse: 'And I will put enmity between you and the woman, and between your offspring and hers; he will crush your head, and you will strike his heel' (Genesis 3:15).

However, in the last chapter of the Bible we read: 'No longer will there be any curse. The throne of God and of the Lamb will be in the city, and his servants will serve him. They will see his face, and his name will be on their foreheads. There will be no more night. They will not need the light of a lamp or the light of the sun, for the Lord God will give them light. And they will reign for ever and ever' (Revelation 22:3–5). Here, again, the word 'hope' is not mentioned, but the nature of hope is clear enough.

I once asked someone why it was that so comparatively little is said about hope. Back came the reply: 'Because it is so often confused with faith, they overlap and people see very little difference between the two'. But there is a great difference. They are not the same thing at all. Today, as much as ever, the subject of hope needs to be held up so that people can consider it in all its many facets. It has seldom been given its rightful place, and yet, as Paul says, while we may grow out of many things as we mature, we never outgrow the need for hope. It remains together with faith and love as one of the three essential elements in our spiritual life. True, love is the greatest and foremost, and faith is justly given considerable emphasis but we neglect hope at our peril. It is vitally important that we possess hope, and that hope must be true. There are enough false hopes going around.

Paul prays in Ephesians 1:18, *GNB:* 'I ask that your minds may be opened to see his light, so that you will know what is the hope to which he has called you.' Through this book I want to share with you that hope which is so essential to us in our daily living.

A light came out of darkness;
No light, no hope had we,
Till Jesus came from Heaven
Our light and hope to be.

(William Hawley *SASB* 94)

THERE IS HOPE FOR EVERYONE!

'Because of the gospel of Jesus Christ we can bodly
proclaim, that whoever you are, and no matter what
your situation is, there is hope for you'

Chapter 1

There is hope for everyone!

THE word 'gospel' means good news. It is derived from an old English word from the 14th Century, 'god spell', where god means good (it still does in the Scandinavian languages) and spell means talk. Gospel today can mean something that is utterly true and correct, and can also refer to the first four books of the New Testament: Matthew, Mark, Luke and John, because they contain good news that it is true and completely reliable. So here is the good news of the gospel: there is hope for everyone!

That surely must be good news! Because of the gospel of Jesus Christ we can boldly proclaim, that whoever you are, and no matter what your situation is, there is hope for you. Putting it another way; no one is hopeless!

Hope with no strings attached? In the business world we all know that there is no such thing as a free meal. Behind every offer in the world of commerce there are usually conditions. When it comes to the gospel, the truth is, there are no strings attached, that is why it is the gospel: good news!

However, it is indisputable that for many the gospel is very difficult to accept at face value. This was true for me. I grew up with the concept of a judgmental God. Unless I lived a holy life, shunned the wrong and did the right, there was no hope for me. Jesus talked about denying self and taking up the cross, so, obviously, if I indulged myself, had a good time, was mildly naughty and essentially selfish, then there was little or no hope for me.

So what about others who really made a mess of their lives? We could always look at them and pronounce, 'There, but for the grace of God, go I', as if to say there is no hope for them, and perhaps for a moment feel that maybe there is still some hope for us if we mend our ways.

The truth is, there is hope, not just for us with our 'small sins', but for everyone who regrets their wrongdoing and intends to change.

In recent years there have been a number of books and television programmes that seek to knock heroes and celebrities from their pedestals. The aim is to reveal a less well-known side to their lives, illustrating their weaknesses and shortcomings. The Bible, in its treatment of its heroes has never hesitated to show both their strong and weak points. In the portrayal of these figures, everything has come to light.

When Oliver Cromwell was going to have his portrait painted, he is reported to have asked the artist, Peter Lely, to paint him 'warts and all'. That is the way the Bible has portrayed its characters. I have only to mention Abraham, who fathered a child, Ishmael, with his servant girl, Hagar, and then sent her away into the desert; Moses, who murdered an Egyptian and had to flee for his life; and King David, who was guilty of adultery and murder, and generally speaking was not a good father.

All these and other personalities in the Scriptures who had 'feet of clay' were key figures in God's plan of salvation. Abraham is remembered as the Father of Faith; Moses as the giver of the Law. Of David we can read this testimony from the Lord, 'I have found David son of Jesse a man after my own heart' (Acts 13:22), and when Jesus came, people referred to him as the Son of David. Now if there was hope for David and the many other people mentioned in the Bible who had blots on their copy book, then there is hope for you and me.

Does it matter how we live, then? Of course it does. Paul wrote in Romans 6:1, 2: 'What shall we say, then? Shall we go on sinning so that grace may increase? By no means!'

God does not come down on us like a ton of bricks when we fail. Moses bore this witness of God in Exodus 34:6: 'The Lord, the Lord, the compassionate and gracious God, slow to anger, abounding in love and faithfulness.' Later, David could echo in Psalm 86:15: 'But you, O Lord, are a compassionate and gracious God, slow to anger, abounding in love and faithfulness.'

God does not condone wrongdoing, knowing that sin enslaves, and eventually brings death and destruction in its path. However the truth remains, that even though we are all sinners, there is still hope. I mentioned previously our 'small sins' and yet there is no such thing as small and big sins in the eyes of an all-holy God. Sin is sin, and all sin comes under the final judgment of God. The wages of sin is death, no matter how we grade the size or seriousness of the sin. So we come back to the opening statement that there is hope for everyone. 'There is no difference, for all have sinned and fall short of the glory of God, and are justified freely by his grace through the redemption that came by Christ Jesus' (Romans 3:22b–24).

In the light of this I would like to raise three questions. Cicero, Roman author, orator and politician said: 'While there is life there is hope.' So my first question refers to this quote. Is it true that while there is life there is hope? Is there a time limit on hope?

Many would say that youth is a time of hope, but if through the years life develops into a complete tragedy, and the approach of the end of life is at hand, is there still hope? If we constantly live a life making wrong choices, going our own way, is there not a point of no return, when the die is cast and the remaining fate of our lives is unavoidable: we have made our bed and we have to lie in it?

Well, the Scriptures suggest that Cicero had it right, and in support of that I refer to the two criminals who were crucified together with Jesus. While one of them cursed Jesus, the other said, 'Jesus, remember me when you come into your Kingdom.'

Jesus answered him: 'I tell you the truth, today you will be with me in paradise' (Luke 23:42, 43).

Think about it, there was nothing else this man could do than to ask Jesus to remember him. He couldn't be of any possible service to the cause of Christ in this life; it was too late for that. He couldn't do as Zacchaeus did, offer to put right any wrongs he had done to others. As the final curtain was falling over his life, he cried out, was heard, and received the promise. Somehow this may not seem fair to some; to wait until the last moments of life without any regard for Christ, and then at the last moment cry out for mercy and receive it.

Yet that was what Jesus taught in the parable of the workers in the vineyard. When some of the workers saw that those who had come late in the day received as much as those who had laboured the whole day, they began to grumble: 'These men who were hired last worked only one hour,' they said, 'and you have made them equal to us who have borne the burden of the work and the heat of the day' (Matthew 20:12). There is a lot more we could say about this parable but I refer to it now only to endorse the fact that through God's love and grace, while there is life there is always hope.

It may seem a contradiction then, when I add that there is always a tragic possibility of a situation arising where there is no hope. This can happen when people become so full of self goodness that they do not see the need for hope. They look at black and say it is white; they look at their own evil lives and say they are righteous; they look at Christ and say he is of the devil. To such people, Jesus says, '"I tell you the truth, all the sins and blasphemies of men will be forgiven them. But whoever blasphemes against the Holy Spirit will never be forgiven; he is guilty of an eternal sin." He said this because they were saying, "He has an evil spirit"' (Mark 3:28–30). Put another way, these people felt they had no need of hope, and when that happens there is likely to be no hope left.

Then there is something else, if there is hope for everyone, will everyone be saved? Will we all see Jesus one day and realise who he is? I mean everyone. To support this statement I again refer to Paul, when he wrote in Philippians 2:10: 'At the name of Jesus every knee should bow, in Heaven and on earth and under the earth, and every tongue confess that Jesus Christ is Lord, to the glory of God the Father.'

Does this mean that everybody will be saved? No! While everyone will meet Jesus, there will be a difference. All will meet the glorified Lord Jesus. Some will meet him as Saviour and Lord. Others will meet him as Lord and Judge. The fact that there is hope for everyone does not mean that everyone will be saved. John 3:16 says most succinctly that Christ died for the whole world, so that whosoever *believes* shall not perish.

This is why there was hope for Abraham, Moses, David, Peter and others. They were sinners, but they believed in God. It affected the direction of their lives, and therefore there was hope. That is why there is hope for you and me as well. By turning to God in faith and allowing him to direct our lives, that hope will be fulfilled because of the offering Christ made on the Cross for the whole world.

Please keep in mind that our God is a God of hope. God prepared our salvation before the foundation of the world was laid, but because he created us with a free will he could not guarantee that we would accept his salvation. God gave his Son, Jesus, as an offering for the whole world, in the hope that we would repent and accept his gift. He made the supreme sacrifice without any guarantee that we would accept it. Like the father in the parable of the prodigal son, who hoped his son would return, and when he did, ran to greet him, so God has his hopes for us. Often his hopes have been in vain as men have rejected him, but still he hopes that we will return. God has hopes for you, don't disappoint him.

When we believe on the Lord Jesus Christ and accept his salvation we notice that hope enters a new dimension for us. There is still hope, but it is different. Before we are saved there *is* hope. When we are saved we *have* hope. I will say more about that later.

HOPE THAT DOES NOT DISAPPOINT.

'When we reach the end of our hoarded resources,
our Father's full giving has only begun'

Chapter 2

Hope that does not disappoint

DO you think Paul could run a four-minute mile? Was Paul serious when he said he could do all things through Christ, a thought which strengthened him? Really? Paul? All things? He seems to make a habit of making controversial claims in his writings and never does things by halves. One moment he claims he is the chief of sinners – not just a sinner, or big sinner, but the chief. The next moment he claims his labours have been more fruitful than all the other apostles. I am not saying he's wrong in making such statements, but perhaps he sometimes exaggerates to make a valid point.

In Romans 5:5, Paul comes out with such a claim which needs some thought before we can accept it. He says, 'Hope does not disappoint us.' Even a passing glance at these words should tell us this statement can't be accepted at face value. Think about it: if anything has the capacity to disappoint, it must be hope. It's in the very nature of the word. If you hope for something, intrinsically there is the possibility of being disappointed. The Salvation Army's songbook reminds us: 'When the woes of life o'ertake me, hopes deceive and fears annoy.'

Hopes placed in family and friends are sooner or later frustrated, and we are so easily disillusioned. Robert Louis Stevenson said, 'To travel hopefully is a better thing than to arrive,' implying that our hopes can often be dashed by reality.

Some people have even been disappointed in Jesus. King Herod for example. In Luke 23:8 we read that when Herod saw Jesus he was greatly pleased, because he had wanted to see him for a long time. He had heard much about him and he wanted to see him

7

perform a miracle. Many people today similarly seek miracles from Jesus, and are similarly disappointed when they fail to be delivered on cue.

Even the disciples' hope in Jesus was disappointed on one occasion at least. In Luke 24:21 we read: 'But we had hoped that he was the one who was going to redeem Israel!' We had hoped ... they said, which implies that they no longer hoped. Jesus was dead and buried and that was the end of it ... or so they thought. They had not understood Jesus and were slow of heart to believe all that the prophets had declared. Their hope was not based on Christ, but upon their own expectations and that is why they were disappointed. Just like Peter who refused to hear Jesus talk about the Cross. Matthew 16:22: 'Peter took him aside and began to rebuke him, "Never, Lord!" he said. "This shall never happen to you!"' But it did, and Peter's hope was shattered.

It is obvious, then, that we can follow Jesus for the wrong reasons. In John 6:26 we read that Jesus said to the people who had sought him out: 'I tell you the truth, you are looking for me, not because you saw miraculous signs but because you ate the loaves and had your fill.' If we follow Jesus out of an unworthy motive, there is every possibility that our hopes will be disappointed.

What, then, are we to make of Paul's statement that hope does not disappoint us? Was he thinking of Isaiah 49:23b: 'Then you will know that I am the Lord; those who hope in me will not be disappointed'? Perhaps, but one thing is clear: Paul was referring to two different types of hope – human and divine.

That there are two such hopes is illustrated in Romans 4:18 regarding Abraham who, 'Against all hope, in hope believed and so became the father of many nations, just as it had been said to him'.

Abraham was promised that he would be the father of nations, with descendants without number, and that through his family the whole world would be blessed. Yet both he and Sarah his wife were old, and such a hope seemed impossible. Human hopes were lost and the situation seemed doomed to failure. However Abraham hung on to hope, a divine hope. A hope that defied human reason and experience, but which nevertheless did not disappoint him.

The prophet Jeremiah reminds us of what God's plan is for us. Jeremiah 29:11 records: '"For I know the plans I have for you," declares the Lord, "plans to prosper you and not to harm you, plans to give you hope and a future."'

Paul again refers to differing hopes in 1 Corinthians 15:32: 'If I fought with wild beasts in Ephesus for merely human reasons, what have I gained? If the dead are not raised, "Let us eat and drink, for tomorrow we die"'.

Sometimes our own hopes can be exhausted, and give way to despair. It is then we have to learn the truth of the lines from the song: 'When we reach the end of our hoarded resources, our Father's full giving has only begun' (*SASB* 579 v. 2)

After the Resurrection of Jesus, the Gospel records that his disciples went out fishing. Naturally with hope, it is in the nature of fishing that we can never know the result before we launch out. We have our hopes, but we simply do not know. The hours went by, yet, try as they might, the disciples did not catch anything. Eventually they headed back to the shore; all hope gone, having caught nothing.

Unexpectedly, Jesus was standing on the shore to greet them. He encouraged them to make one more attempt. The disciples were worn out, without any more hope, but then Christ came with a plea that they should try once more. It was enough! They received new hope, a hope that defied logic. Every fibre in their bodies said, 'Enough is enough, let's call it a day!' But they tried once more for the last time and they were not disappointed!

We need to have that same hope motivate us to follow God's will for our lives, even though, humanly speaking, we cannot see where it will take us. If we have a hope based not on our own expectations, resources or understanding but on the words of Jesus, then we have a hope that will not disappoint us.

Jesus said in John 14:2, 3: 'In my Father's house are many rooms; if it were not so, I would have told you. I am going there to prepare a place for you. And if I go and prepare a place for you, I will come back and take you to be with me that you also may be where I am.'

This is the hope that the glorified Jesus has given us, and one day, when we gather on the other side of the river, and hear the voice of many angels, numbering thousands upon thousands, and ten thousand times ten thousand; when we see him seated on the throne and give him blessing and honour and glory and might forever and ever; when we see Abraham and Jacob and all the prophets, and when we see people come from the East and West, and from the North and the South and sit down in the Kingdom of God: when we ourselves are among the ransomed of the Lord who come to Zion with singing; everlasting joy, and gladness, and find that sorrow and sighing shall flee away; when we see a great multitude that no one can count, from every nation, from all tribes and peoples and languages, standing before the throne and before the Lamb, robed in white, with palm branches in their hands; when we hear the angelic choir sing with full voice, 'Worthy is the Lamb that was slain to receive power and wealth and wisdom and might and honour and glory and blessing', then we will fully understand and can turn to each other and say: 'This is far greater and more wonderful than we had hoped for.' Until that day we can sing Charles Wesley's words:

> *Let us see thy great salvation,*
> *Perfectly restored in thee.*
> *Changed from glory into glory,*
> *Till in Heaven we take our place,*
> *Till we cast our crowns before thee,*
> *Lost in wonder, love and praise.*

(SASB 438 v. 3)

That's a hope that will not disappoint!

HOPE WHEN THINGS GO TERRIBLY WRONG.

'There are endless possibilities for life to go wrong,
and for many people it does. Is it possible to
keep hope alive when life can be so cruel?'

Chapter 3

Hope when things go terribly wrong

'YESTERDAY, all my troubles seemed so far away' – so begins Paul McCartney's plaintive song 'Yesterday'. Most people begin their lives with hopes and dreams for the future. This is how it should be, and if at an early age we possess a faith and hope in God, then we have every reason to be optimistic. But what if everything goes wrong and our best hopes are brutally dashed and we long for 'yesterday' so we can begin again?

This is the real-life situation for millions of people around the world. People get married, with their dreams and hopes, then it all ends with an ugly divorce. They prepare for a useful life, then get struck down by a crippling illness. They raise their children, only to see them destroyed by drugs. Every day we read of murders where the victim has done nothing to deserve such a fate except be in the wrong place at the wrong time.

There are endless possibilities for life to go wrong, and for many people it does. 'That's life!' some people will say. 'Get real. Life is tough. Life isn't fair.' If this is true, what value has hope in our lives?

The apostle Paul had more than his fair share of problems yet had an outlook on life which enabled him to say in Romans 8:28: 'We know that in all things God works for the good of those who love him, who have been called according to his purpose.' Even so the question remains: is it possible to keep hope alive when life can be so cruel?

The Old Testament character of Joseph was such a person. His childhood was filled with hope and dreams. His life was filled with promise, but it all went dreadfully wrong. First, his brothers turned on him. They almost murdered him, but settled for selling him into a life of slavery instead. This did not crush Joseph's optimism, and even as a slave he did his best. Installed in the house of Potiphar, he soon built up a relationship of trust, and was made steward, with responsibility for running the household.

Unfortunately, Joseph was falsely accused by Potiphar's wife and again narrowly escaped death, ending up in prison instead. Even here he kept up a positive attitude. He did his best to help his fellow prisoners, but one whom he had helped quickly forgot about him the moment he returned to his former position. Left in a jail to rot, Joseph could easily have become depressed and tempted to give up all hope. Psalm 42:11 surely expresses what he and many others have experienced: 'Why are you downcast, O my soul? Why so disturbed within me? Put your hope in God, for I will yet praise him, my Saviour and my God.'

Then suddenly Joseph's life changes completely. From the utmost deprivation he is exalted to a position of prestige and power. Many novels have been written with this kind of dramatic development. An innocent man is thrown into prison, or exiled for many years, eventually coming back, bringing retribution and revenge in his path, like the classic story of Ben Hur.

In Alexander Dumas's novel, *The Count of Monte Cristo*, the hero, Edmund Dantes, is cheated of his fortune and spends 14 years in prison. While in prison, he learns the whereabouts of a secret cache of treasure and on his escape he is restored to a position of wealth and power. He then devotes his life to wreaking revenge upon those who betrayed him. But the story of Joseph is not fiction. Joseph is truly in a position of wealth and power where he has the ability, if he wishes, to avenge those who have afflicted him — his brothers for selling him into slavery, Potiphar's wife for her lies and treachery, Pharoah's servant who Joseph had helped and who promptly forgot him when he was restored to his former position of service.

Now he can effect righteous judgment, but he doesn't. Revenge is sweet, it is said, but God's word says: 'Do not take revenge, my friends, but leave room for God's wrath, for it is written: "It is mine to avenge; I will repay," says the Lord' (Romans 12:19).

When Joseph's brothers discover what has happened they naturally fear the worst. Joseph, however, reacts in a way they could never have anticipated. And later on, after their father's death, confirming the hope that had sustained him throughout his life, he says of their treatment of him: 'You meant evil against me; but God meant it for good' (Genesis 50:20, *NKJV*).

It took the brothers some time before it sank in and they could accept the wonder of the situation. Not only were they forgiven, their worst deeds had been turned around into something positive. What a relief! What joy!

This is the message of hope we have in Christ. Ours is not a God of hate and vengeance, but of love and forgiveness. A God of hope! No matter what happens to us in this life, God can turn it into something good. There is always hope for the one who believes.

Samuel Brengle was a young Salvation Army officer in America. In the 1890s an opponent of the movement threw a brick at Brengle, hitting him on the back of the head. Brengle was confined to bed for a long period of convalescence. During this period he wrote the book, *Helps to Holiness.* It was to be the first of many books on holiness, and opened up a whole new ministry to him; a ministry which continues to this day as many of his writings are in print, or can be read on the internet. Later in life, reflecting on the incident, he said, 'If it hadn't been for the brick there would not have been the book.' He could have quoted Joseph: 'You meant it for evil, but God meant it for good.'

George Marshall was a Salvationist living in Northern England. Soon after his marriage, an accident down a coal mine broke his back, leaving him paralysed for the rest of his life. A tragedy; but because George could no longer work down the mine he was able to begin composing music instead. From his pen flowed music which has been a source of inspiration and blessing for many.

There are countless other examples of evil being turned to good, but the greatest example of all is to be seen in the life Jesus himself.

Condemned to die on a cross, it seemed his enemy was triumphant. But what the enemy meant for evil, God meant for good, for the sake of the whole world. Through the death and resurrection of Christ we all have ground for hope – a living hope, so that no matter what other hopes are dashed, no matter what personal tragedy strikes us, the hope we have in Christ stands sure. It was this kind of hope that sustained Joseph in his trials, and it will sustain us too.

> *Leave God to order all thy ways,*
> *And hope in him whate'er betide;*
> *Thou'lt find him in the evil days*
> *Thy all-sufficient strength and guide;*
> *Who trusts in God's unchanging love*
> *Builds on the rock that naught can move.*

(George Christian Neumark *SASB* 738 v. 1)

HOPE FOR TODAY.

'I am the resurrection and the life' (John 11:25).
Not: 'I will be' or 'I was' but 'I am'

18

Chapter 4

Hope for today

CICERO said, 'While there is life, there is hope', so presumably the alternative also applies: where there is no longer life, there is no longer hope. When Lazarus the brother of Martha and Mary died, it would seem hope died with him. Jesus, who could have saved the situation, delayed his arrival until it was too late. Both Martha and Mary, independently of each other, greeted Jesus with the same sad words: 'Lord, if you had been here, my brother would not have died.' But Martha also added, 'But I know that even now God will give you whatever you ask' (John 11:21, 22, 32).

Why did she say that? Did she still have hope, even after death? As if to strengthen her hope Jesus said to her, 'Your brother will rise again.' It would appear that Martha still held out hope for Lazarus, but it was a remote hope for the distant future. Martha answered, 'I know he will rise again in the resurrection at the last day.'

Many people have the same kind of hope as Martha: a hope placed in the distant future and not relevant for today. Many criticise this kind of hope as: 'Pie in the sky when you die'. They write off Christianity as irrelevant for life today, as insurance for an unknown future, and that's all. Many counter that jibe by saying, 'We have meat on the plate while we wait!' Jesus said the hope we have for tomorrow affects the way we live today, declaring: 'I am the resurrection and the life' (John 11:25). Not: 'I will be' or 'I was' but 'I am'. Jesus Christ is the same yesterday and today and forever, and he is relevant now. This was the lesson Martha and Mary had to learn, and perhaps we do too.

So it was that Jesus laid down the challenge. If you truly have a hope for eternity it ought to affect your faith and action today. The problem was that Lazarus was dead, and a stone sealed him in his tomb. Then Jesus shocked and challenged everyone present. 'Take away the stone,' he said.

In view of who Jesus was, this might seem a strange request in more ways than one. After all, Jesus was the Son of God. If he wanted the stone moved, couldn't he do it himself? He was about to raise Lazarus from the dead, surely moving the stone was nothing in comparison. He who could raise the dead could easily move the stone single-handed.

But here we have a spiritual lesson. Martha and Mary were given the opportunity to prove their faith. Were they willing to move the stone which hid things they would rather not see? It would appear that Jesus wants to work with us and through us, not just for us. He doesn't do what we can do for ourselves. We can't raise the dead, but we can move the stone. Does our eternal hope decide what we do today? Jesus said, 'Did I not tell you that if you believed, you would see the glory of God?' So they rolled away the stone, and Jesus rewarded their faith.

It is a good thing to hope in God to secure the world to come, but Jesus wants that eternal hope to be reflected in the way we live today by being willing to meet the challenge and, in faith, moving away the stone that hides what we rather would not see — the stone which prevents Jesus performing miracles and bringing new life into a hopeless situation.

At the beginning of 1888, more than 120 years ago, The Salvation Army commenced work in a deprived district of Oslo, Norway. That same year they erected a building containing a hall that could seat 700 people, a national headquarters and a training college for cadets. It was to serve The Salvation Army in Norway for the next 90 years before being demolished to make way for a new ring road. The thing was, in 1888 there was no nationwide army, just a movement in its pure infancy with a handful of centres. But they erected the building in faith, and their faith was not in vain. They had a hope. Some would have said 'What a hope!', but God honoured it. They could build a headquarters, but only God could build an army, and he did.

The same thing happened in country after country. Five years previously, in 1883, Major and Mrs Francis Simmonds and Lieutenant Alice Teeger arrived in Cape Town, South Africa, to commence the work of The Salvation Army there. The press had heard that The Salvation Army was coming to South Africa and turned up to see them arrive. They were puzzled when only a married couple and a young girl disembarked from the ship. 'Where are your soldiers?' they asked. 'We are going to raise them here,' was the answer. That was their hope and their faith was rewarded.

This is the point! It is our hope for tomorrow that gives us faith for today. That was what Jesus said to the people gathered at the grave of Lazarus. 'Did I not tell you that if you believed, you would see the glory of God?' said Jesus. The truth is that when we do not have hope, hope for tomorrow, then we lose our faith for today. We cease to act because we have lost hope. The wonderful truth is that Jesus gives us a living hope. We have a hope, something to look forward to on that last day, and this gives us faith for today and by that faith we can experience his glory now!

> *What a work the Lord has done*
> *By his saving grace;*
> *Let us praise him, every one,*
> *In his holy place.*

> (Albert Orsborn *SASB* 769 v. 1)

HOPE AGAINST HOPE.

"Hope ceases to be something we do and becomes something we possess."

Chapter 5

Hope against hope

WHAT is the first thing we stop doing when we become Christians? Sinning? No, we stop hoping! Hope ceases to be something we *do* and becomes something we *possess*. The writer to the Hebrews encourages us to hold unswervingly to the hope we profess (see Hebrews 10:23).

On the first Easter Sunday two disciples were walking along the road to Emmaus. They were full of sorrow and confessed to one they thought was a stranger, referring to Jesus, 'We had hoped that he was the one who was going to redeem Israel' (Luke 24:21). Later, as they shared an evening meal with that 'stranger' he revealed to them that he was, in fact, Jesus, and Luke relates that they returned at once to Jerusalem. Upon arrival they did not say, 'We had stopped hoping, but now we are hoping again.' No, they said, 'It is true!' They had experienced the living Christ and hope had changed its character. It was no longer just something they did, it had become something they had.

I'm speaking of the hope that comes from knowing Christ. There is another type of hope, we could call it a temporal hope. Both these types of hope can exist side by side, but it is important to know the difference. Paul refers to both kinds in his writings. To the Christians in Rome he wrote: 'I hope to visit you while passing through' (Romans 15:24b). This is temporal hope, and can refer to something that is uncertain. Later in the same letter he writes: 'Be joyful in hope' (Romans 12:12). This is not temporal, uncertain hope. How could an uncertain hope give us joy? It is not Paul saying. 'I am hoping for the best.' He is saying hope is something you can possess and which gives joy.

23

When I was a child, like any other child I became excited as Christmas approached. I knew I would be getting some presents. I didn't just hope for presents, I knew I would receive some. Such was my confidence in my parents and family. Even so, there was an element of hope, simply because I didn't know everything, and that excited me.

In the same way, we who belong to Jesus have a hope. Jesus said, 'If you, then, though you are evil, know how to give good gifts to your children, how much more will your Father in Heaven give good gifts to those who ask him!' (Matthew 7:11).

We know Jesus has gone ahead of us to prepare the way and a place for us; such is our confidence and faith in him. We know so much, we just don't know everything. Here is the element of hope. It is not a question of whether there is more to existence than just this life, it is the sure and certain hope that when time ends for us, we have an eternity in the Kingdom of God to look forward to, and this gives us joy.

We must bear in mind that joy is much more than happiness. The word happiness is derived from the word hap, meaning luck, chance. Therefore happiness is often dependent upon outward circumstances over which we do not have full control. If life is treating us well, good things are happening to us, then we are said to be happy. The joy of which we speak is based not on what is happening around us, but what is happening inside us. True joy can be affected by outward circumstances, but it is not dependent upon them. Because of the joy that our certain hope gives us, we can be joyful even in times of trouble, as Paul confirms in 2 Corinthians 7:4b: 'I am greatly encouraged; in all our troubles my joy knows no bounds.'

We are exhorted to grow in the grace and knowledge of our Lord and Saviour Jesus Christ, and we learn increasingly as our pilgrimage on earth continues, but no matter how much we learn, and no matter how strong our faith, there will always be something we do not know, that will always remain a mystery.

To quote Paul in 1 Corinthians 13:12: 'Now we see but a poor reflection as in a mirror; then we shall see face to face. Now I know in part; then I shall know fully, even as I am fully known.' This ignorance of the future does not produce fear but hope, and the hope we possess does not diminish with the years, but grows, and with it so does our joy. So we do not need to be like those who go through life just hoping for the best, because we know we possess a wonderful hope, filling us with joy. Thank God for that!

GREAT LOVE,
SMALL HOPES.

'The one thing he had hoped for was being denied him
He could not understand that his father's love and
provision was so much greater than
he could ever imagine.'

Chapter 6

Great love, small hopes

THE thing that got his goat, and which was the last straw for him, was the fattened calf. The servants knew it would annoy him, and were not slow in telling him. It was, after all, the one thing he hoped for — to have a party with his friends, and now it was being used to celebrate his younger brother's homecoming. No wonder he was upset. The one thing he had hoped for was being denied him. He could not understand that his father's love and provision was so much greater than he could ever imagine.

We can read about it in Luke 15. Many people, when they read the parable commonly referred to as the Parable of the Prodigal Son, do just that: they reflect on the restoration of the prodigal son. But Jesus did not tell this story just to say there was hope for the prodigal; he wanted to tell us that there was hope for both sons, because of the father's great love.

Let's look at the parable again through the eyes of hope. Briefly, the younger of two sons leaves his father and goes into a distant country. The original hearers of this parable would understand the symbolism of that simple statement. There is an interesting reference in the story of Naaman who came to the prophet Elisha to be healed. Afterwards, Naaman came with an unusual request: 'Please let me, your servant, be given as much earth as a pair of mules can carry, for your servant will never again make burnt offerings and sacrifices to any other god but the Lord' (2 Kings 5:17).

In Naaman's day it was generally believed that gods were closely connected to particular lands. Therefore, because Naaman wanted to continue to worship the God of Israel, he wanted to take some earth from Israel back home so that when he knelt in worship he could do it on Israel's land. When Jews arrived at the borders of Israel, having been abroad, they took off their sandals and shook them. Why? They did not wish to pollute their holy land with the gods of other lands. It may be recalled that when the disciples were sent out to evangelise, Jesus said, 'If any place will not welcome you or listen to you, shake the dust off your feet when you leave, as a testimony against them' (Mark 6:11). What kind of testimony was that? It was to show that they were outside the Kingdom of God.

So when the younger son departed to a distant country, it meant not only that he had left his own country but also that he had forsaken God. To begin with it seemed that everything was fine, but eventually he became poor and lonely. He had set out with everything but wasted it all in senseless living and he was left without money and without friends, alone with his regrets and despair. In his misery he remembered his home and his family.

How many people have turned around their lives by the inspiration of childhood memories? So it was that hope was kindled. A hope that told him that there must be something better in life than what he was experiencing. Not everyone who deserts God ends up in the gutter. Many prosper in the ways of the world, but still come to a point when they realise it is meaningless. There must be something more, something better. So with the son in the parable, he repented and returned home hoping for a job as a servant.

Here comes the turning point in the story. There is no resentful father pointing the condemning finger and declaring, 'What did I say? You have brought this on yourself. You made your bed and now you must lie in it.' Far from gloating over his repentant son, the father runs to greet him, hugs him, and without giving him a period of probation to see if he is really sorry, immediately gives him three things: a robe, a ring and shoes. In other words his sonship is restored to him.

The garment meant righteousness, the ring meant authority and the shoes, freedom. The black slaves in the American South had no shoes. They used to sing, 'I've got shoes ... when I get to Heaven, gonna put on my shoes, gonna walk all over God's Heaven.' That was their hope! In this life they were slaves, but freedom was coming.

The wonderful truth here is that God does not expect us to grovel in the dust, begging him to give us a job, anything. After all, look what he did to make it possible for us to return to him. 'God demonstrates his own love for us in this: while we were still sinners, Christ died for us. Since we have now been justified by his blood, how much more shall we be saved from God's wrath through him!' (Romans 5:8, 9).

If God did all that to save us from our own selfish living, then he is hardly likely to hesitate in welcoming us home when we turn to him. 'Today you will be with me' is not just a promise to the dying thief on the cross; it is wonderfully true for us too. He accepts us gladly and immediately when we turn to him in faith. That is what the prodigal did. Then the party started.

This brings us back to the older son who had never strayed from home. He was the dutiful son, who did not waste his resources in riotous living. His great hope was the fattened calf! When he came home from working in the fields, he was informed by the servants of what was happening. They did not mention the robe, ring or shoes, just the fattened calf (Luke 15:27).

That did it! The stay-at-home son's hope for a chance of using the fattened calf to have a party with his friends was gone. It was just a bagatelle, really, compared to everything else that was happening. Yet the father who had welcomed home the prodigal with such extravagance, showed the same love to both sons. 'My son,' the father said, 'you are always with me, and everything I have is yours.'

Charles Dickens wrote a novel titled *Great Expectations*. This parable could be better called *Small Expectations and Great Love*. The younger son hoped for a place among the servants. The older son hoped for a calf. They were both wrong. The father's love far exceeded both hopes. I can recall a Sunday school teacher commenting on the Lord's Prayer, saying, 'We are taught to pray for our daily bread, not cake. God has promised to give us what we need, not what we want.' This is in great contrast to the words of Jesus in John 10:10: 'I have come that they may have life, and have it to the full.' Even the psalmist realised that we have a generous God. 'You prepare a table before me in the presence of my enemies. You anoint my head with oil; my cup overflows' (Psalm 23 v. 5).

In the economy of things, because of God's love, we too have far more to look forward to than we can imagine. We may have our hopes, but they fall pitifully short of the glory that God, because of his great love, has prepared for us. As Paul wrote: 'No eye has seen, no ear has heard, no mind has conceived what God has prepared for those who love him' (1 Corinthians 2:9).

This is the ground of our hope: God's unbounded and unlimited love for us. This is best revealed in Paul's statement: 'While we were still sinners, Christ died for us. Since we have now been justified by his blood, how much more shall we be saved from God's wrath through him!' (Romans 5:8,9). This is great stuff, really good news. Whatever hopes we may or may not have for the future, God has prepared something even greater.

Then how much more shall God our Father
In love forgive, in love forgive!
Then how much more shall God our Father
Our wants supply, and none deny!

(John Gowans *SASB* 50, chorus).

HOPE, THE SOURCE OF OUR JOY.

'Something to do. something to love.
and something to hope for'

32

Chapter 7

Hope, the source of our joy

JOSEPH ADDISON declared that the 'three grand essentials to happiness in this life are something to do, something to love, and something to hope for'. How profound are these words. Being idle because nobody has use for you is soul destroying. Having a challenge and a task is wonderful, but simply having a job to go to can work wonders. William Booth realised this in the early days of The Salvation Army and established labour bureaux to meet that need. The principle of work is built into the fabric of our Army.

Addison's second point is equally true: we need someone who cares about us and whom we love. It is impossible to be unloved and happy.

Finally Addison says we need something to hope for. You may have heard the story of the man who had recently moved into an old peoples' home, who received a visit. 'How do you like living here?' a visitor asked him. 'It's fine,' the new resident replied. 'The people are nice and the food is good, but there's no future here.'

We need something to look forward to. We who belong to the Lord have reason to be thankful that we have these three elements included in our faith. We can serve the Lord, know his love and face the future with hope. Paul summed it all up when he said in 1 Thessalonians 1:3: 'We continually remember before our God and Father your work produced by faith, your labour prompted by love, and your endurance inspired by hope in our Lord Jesus Christ.'

Throughout my life I have constantly been fully aware of the joy that comes from these three elements. There has always been plenty to do, my life has been filled with love and there has always been something to look forward to. I praise God for that. However, if you had asked me in the early days of my life what it was that gave me the greatest sense of joy, I would have answered it was the knowledge that I had been used by God to bless others. As Proverbs 11:25 puts it, 'He who refreshes others will himself be refreshed.'

However some things have changed in my outlook and thinking and I would answer that question differently today. There is an incident recorded in Luke 10 where 72 disciples of Jesus were sent out on a campaign to prepare the way for their Lord. They were given specific instructions on what to do, and off they went. The Gospel says nothing about their mood when they set out, but they were moving out of their comfort zone, so there must surely have been a degree of trepidation.

However it was a different story when they returned. There was the joy of meeting Jesus and each other again. They had so much to report. Not the least was the fact that they had experienced spiritual victories. They were exuberant, and in a triumphant mood. Jesus confirmed that they had made inroads into the devil's kingdom. Even so, in the midst of all the excitement and celebration over having experienced being a spiritual blessing to others, and the joy it gave them in return, Jesus adds something else by saying, 'However, do not rejoice that the spirits submit to you, but rejoice that your names are written in Heaven' (Luke 10:20).

The concept of a book in which God has recorded the names of the faithful is not a new one. It is referred to in the time of Moses, when he prayed: 'But now, please forgive their sin — but if not, then blot me out of the book you have written' (Exodus 32:32).

This is a tremendous prayer with an element of prophecy in it. Moses is willing to have his name blotted out of God's book in order that others might be forgiven. Moses could not see that prayer answered in his life, but one greater than Moses achieved that, when Jesus died on the Cross. There are also references to a

34

book of life in the Psalms and in Revelation. Now, why did Jesus refer to this while his disciples were rejoicing over what had been accomplished. What's that all about?

In the *King James Version* of the Bible the phrase, 'and it came to pass' appears 497 times. It's a good phrase because it is a reminder that everything we experience in life comes and passes. That can be a comfort in times of sorrow, but we need this reminder in times of joyful exuberance as well. How excited football fans can become when their team wins! They sing and cheer, but their celebrations often only last a week or so until the next match! I think the only football result that is universally remembered in England is the 1966 World Cup Final!

Jesus needed to remind his disciples, and us, that although there are great spiritual joys to be experienced in this life, they too will pass. Take the joy of finding salvation for example. If, after a lifetime of following Christ, the only thing you remember is the day you got saved, then something is wrong. True, that is a great experience, but it is only the beginning. Life moves on, and God has much more in store for us. This applies to everything we experience – 'and it came to pass'.

Things do not remain the same and we cannot live on past blessings. Jesus is saying that, no matter what you experience in this life, there is always something better ahead. We never need to peak in the spiritual life. We never have to long for the past to return. God always has something better prepared for us. Always! What is even more tremendous is the fact that it is a personal promise: 'Rejoice that your names are written in Heaven.'

You cannot imagine that! 'No eye has seen, no ear has heard, no mind has conceived what God has prepared for those who love him' (1 Corinthians 2:9). Whatever it is God has prepared, it has got your name on it.

Of course there is still a lot to do in this life, here and now. Like the disciples, we are called to go out and prepare the people for Jesus. Like them, we are called to serve him, and like them there will be times of celebration over victories won, and perhaps tears, like Peter shed on one occasion. However, let us not be like those who look back and say,

> *Those were the days my friend,*
> *I thought they'd never end.*

Rather, let us be like Paul, who as he approached the end of his life could write:

'I have fought the good fight, I have finished the race, I have kept the faith. Now there is in store for me the crown of righteousness, which the Lord, the righteous Judge, will award to me on that day — and not only to me, but also to all who have longed for his appearing' (2 Timothy 4:7,8). The best is yet to be. That is our hope. That is our joy.

> *Let nothing draw me back*
> *Or turn my heart from thee,*
> *But by the Calvary track*
> *Bring me at last to see*
> *The courts of God, that city fair,*
> *And find my name is written there.*

(Albert Orsborn SASB 59 v. 4).

THE GROUND AND NATURE OF OUR HOPE!

'The hope that does not disappoint, the hope that
sustains us when all else fails, the hope that
is still there when this life ebbs away.'

Chapter 8

The ground and nature of our hope

'ALWAYS be prepared to give an answer to everyone who asks you to give the reason for the hope that you have,' wrote Peter in his first letter (3:15). Now, that is good advice to every Christian, and while we may have our own personal reason for possessing hope, there is one common ground for us to build our hope on. One source, if you will. You might say that Jesus is the ground of our hope, and that's partly correct, but not completely. The ultimate source of our hope comes from somewhere else. It may be a surprise when I do not refer to Jesus as the ultimate ground of our hope, but Jesus himself referred to an authority outside of himself. In John 7:16 Jesus declared: 'My teaching is not my own. It comes from him who sent me.' In John 6:38 Jesus said, 'For I have come down from Heaven not to do my will but to do the will of him who sent me.'

Bear in mind that the love of God and the hope that it gives was known in the world before Christ came. Psalm 23 is an example of this. Here David describes God as a shepherd who loves him and cares for him. Christ was later to identify himself as the Good Shepherd. In the first half of the psalm David reflects over God's love:

> 'He makes me lie down in green pastures,
>   he leads me beside quiet waters,
> he restores my soul.
>   He guides me in paths of righteousness
>   for his name's sake.'

Then in the remainder of the psalm he expresses the hope that this love gives.

> 'Even though I walk
> through the valley of the shadow of death,
> I will fear no evil,
> for you are with me;
> your rod and your staff,
> they comfort me.
>
> You prepare a table before me
> in the presence of my enemies.
> You anoint my head with oil;
> my cup overflows.
>
> Surely goodness and love will follow me
> all the days of my life,
> and I will dwell in the house of the Lord
> forever.'

All this has to do with hope, and the source of the hope is the love of God.

Therefore the ultimate ground of our hope is to be found in the love of God. What does the Gospel say? Jesus so loved the world that he came? No: 'For God so loved the world that he gave his one and only Son, that whoever believes in him shall not perish but have eternal life' (John 3:16).

You see, in his teachings, Jesus explained the love of God. He talked about the Resurrection to his disciples so that they would not be completely crushed when they saw him die on the Cross, even though they did not understand what was happening at the time.

His life gives us hope. His Resurrection is the proof, if it were needed, that the hope he gave us was not a vain hope, but a living and effectual hope. If, for example, a man declared his love to his beloved, and to prove his love jumped into a swollen river and died, it might prove how great love his love was, but at the same time prove how useless and wasted it was. Jesus by dying on the Cross demonstrated his love for us, but if there were no Resurrection how useless and wasteful it would be!

Jesus, by his life and death, revealed his love, but the hope he gives us comes through his Resurrection. It was transforming and redeeming. So the ultimate ground of the hope we possess — the hope that does not disappoint, the hope that sustains us when all else fails, the hope that grows greater as our memories become more distant, the hope that is still there when this life ebbs away — is God's love, experienced in the Old Testament, but taught by Jesus and revealed fully through his life and death.

Peter in the opening verses of his first letter (1:3) speaks of a living hope available to all believers. He says the ground of our hope comes from God, and adds that the content of this hope is found in the Resurrection of Jesus Christ. What we see in the Resurrection of Jesus is the living hope that God has given to us. The Jesus of the Resurrection is the same Jesus who lived on the earth, but he is different. What he is now, we will become. This is the nature of the hope we possess.

What conclusions can we arrive at from what the Bible tells us of the resurrected Christ? Well, he had a body; he was not a ghost or simply a spirit. To emphasise this, on one of his first appearances to the disciples, he asked for and ate some fish. He had a body, but it was not subject to the physical laws of this world. He could appear at will, even in a room that was locked and barred. He could also disappear from sight in the same way.

Jesus made no attempt to explain his Resurrection, he simply manifested it. His resurrected body was immortal. Lazarus was brought back to life from the dead, but he was not immortal. He eventually died. Jesus lives! His mortality took on immortality, his body remained recognisable, but it was fundamentally different. This explains the kind of hope we possess.

The Christian creeds state that we believe not only in the immortality of the soul, but in the resurrection of the body. Like

Jesus we can look forward to a new body. We will be recognisable, but different. Peter adds that this hope should fill us with joy, even though at present we are beset with difficulties, trials and infirmities. These setbacks are like a fire that purifies us until the day of Christ's return. They form and prepare us, so that we grow spiritually, not *despite* the trials that come to us in life, but *because* of them. We come through these experiences strengthened in the hope we possess.

What we are being prepared for is a mystery. Peter and Paul agree on this. Peter speaks of an inheritance that can never perish, spoil or fade – kept in Heaven for you (1 Peter 1:4, 5). Paul, in 1 Corinthians 13, refers to knowing in part, and seeing through a glass darkly, compared to the full revelation to come. The fact is, we do not know what form our hope will take when we enter eternity, but we have the promise of Jesus that we will be with him. That should be sufficient!

WHY WE NEED HOPE.

'When I surveyed what I had toiled to achieve, everything
was meaningless, a chasing after the wind;
nothing was gained under the sun.'

Chapter 9

Why we need hope

HAVING spent a large part of my life in Norway, I have come to realise that Norwegians have an innate understanding of the meaning of hope. This is because they live in a land which has a long, hard, cold and, not least, dark winter. In the far north of the country the sun never appears for about two months during the winter. I am reminded of C. S. Lewis's book, *The Lion, the Witch and the Wardrobe*. In it he describes the fictional world of Narnia, where it is constantly winter and Christmas never comes. That sounds pretty hopeless to me, whereas in the darkness of winter everybody in Norway looks forward to Christmas, and just before it arrives they greet the news that the sun has turned and they are once again moving towards brighter times. It is this hope that helps them hold out in the darkness. Outwardly, very little changes to begin with, but the hope of summer and sun sustains them.

It is not only Norwegians who experience days of darkness. Such days come to all of us at periods in our lives, and we need hope to get us through them. Without it we would simply give up and die.

So we need hope to help us through the dark days, when life doesn't make sense or when life doesn't seem fair. The Old Testament tells us that Naomi, her husband and two sons emigrated in the hope of a better life. In a strange country, her husband and two sons die, and she is left with two daughters-in-law. She is overwhelmed by the disaster that has overtaken her, and tells them to return to their own people and she will do the same. One daughter-in-law, Ruth, refuses to leave Naomi, and together they return to Naomi's family in Canaan.

'"Don't call me Naomi," she told them, "call me Mara, because the Almighty has made my life very bitter. I went away full, but the Lord has brought me back empty"' (Ruth 1:20, 21).

Life didn't make sense for Naomi, and it would have been impossible for anyone, there and then, to explain it all, yet God was working out his plan of salvation through Naomi, and there was hope for her, as she later discovered. We don't always understand why everything happens to us the way it does, and therefore we need hope.

We need hope when God seems to hide his face. That's what happened to Job. In Job's book we read, 'But if I go to the east, he is not there; if I go to the west, I do not find him. When he is at work in the north, I do not see him; when he turns to the south, I catch no glimpse of him. But he knows the way that I take; when he has tested me, I will come forth as gold' (Job 23:8–10).

But Job could also say: 'I know that my Redeemer lives, and that in the end he will stand upon the earth. And after my skin has been destroyed, yet in my flesh I will see God; I myself will see him with my own eyes – I, and not another. How my heart yearns within me!' (Job 19:25–27) This is hope, and it sustained Job. We too need hope!

We need hope because we cannot see the end from the beginning. Romans 8:24 reminds us that it is in hope that we are saved, but hope that is seen is no hope at all. Who hopes for what he already has?

We need hope because we cannot understand everything. This may be because we are not ready to know. As there is a lot a child cannot know until he or she reaches an age of maturity, so there are things we cannot know without the help of time. Jesus said to his disciples in John 16:12: 'I have much more to say to you, more than you can now bear.' To which Paul comments in 1 Corinthians 13:11b,12: 'When I became a man, I put childish ways behind me. Now we see but a poor reflection as in a mirror; then we shall see face to face. Now I know in part; then I shall know fully, even as I am fully known'. We need this hope.

46

We need hope because this life alone doesn't satisfy the human soul. The book of Ecclesiastes (2:11) puts it like this: 'Yet when I surveyed all that my hands had done and what I had toiled to achieve, everything was meaningless, a chasing after the wind; nothing was gained under the sun.'

People are constantly looking for something new, which is symptomatic of the fact that they are dissatisfied with what they already have. They want something more. Today people are obsessed with excitement, be it shopping, gambling, football, sex. But at the end of the day they are still dissatisfied. How different it is for those of us of the household of faith!

Of course we delight in the good things life provides, but we realise there is more, and that can be summed up in the living hope we have in Christ. This is so powerful, that even as life ebbs away we can be possessed of that hope. Paul's words as translated in the *King James Version* of 2 Timothy 4:6–8 express this clearly: 'For I am now ready to be offered, and the time of my departure is at hand. I have fought a good fight, I have finished my course, I have kept the faith: Henceforth there is laid up for me a crown of righteousness, which the Lord, the righteous judge, shall give me at that day: and not to me only, but unto all them also that love his appearing.' We need this hope.

Each day is a journey into the unknown, and at times we feel lost. Like Thomas we say: 'Lord, we don't know where you are going, so how can we know the way?' Jesus answers: 'I am the way ...' (John 14:5, 6).

When we stand beside a grave with mixed emotions like Mary and Martha, Jesus says: 'I am the resurrection and the life' (John 11:25). Confronted as we are by the brevity of life, and tempted like Job to say, 'My days are swifter than a weaver's shuttle, and they come to an end without hope. Remember, O God, that my life is but a breath; my eyes will never see happiness again' (Job 7:6, 7), Jesus says: 'In my Father's house are many rooms; if it were not so, I would have told you. I am going there to prepare a place for you' (John 14:2).

We need hope, otherwise we would simply give up. My father made a puzzle once by cutting up a pattern of squares, like a draughtboard, into various shapes. We had it for years and never managed to put it back together. It seemed impossible, yet we knew it was possible. Then one day, after many years, our son found the solution. We could hardly believe it. After so many attempts over so many years, the pieces finally came together; the puzzle was solved. If my father had said that it could not be done we would have given up much earlier and thrown the pieces away.

That is what people do with life, when they have no hope they give up and throw the pieces away. But we have a Heavenly Father who says there is an answer to the puzzle of life. One day we will see the pieces come together and that which has been a mystery will be made clear. Like Jesus our Saviour, we will not give up until it is accomplished.

We need hope. We have hope.

Praise be to the God and Father of our Lord Jesus Christ! In his great mercy he has given us new birth into a living hope through the Resurrection of Jesus Christ from the dead.

And I shall see him face to face,
And tell the story, saved by grace.

(Fanny Crosby *SASB* chorus 245).

HOPE AND LIFESTYLE.

'People who were well known for a Godless way of life,
changed completely, to the amazement of
family, friends and the local community.'

Chapter 10

Hope and lifestyle

'DEAR friends, now we are children of God, and what we will be has not yet been made known. But we know that when he appears, we shall be like him, for we shall see him as he is' (1 John 3:2).

One of the results of possessing Christian hope is that our lifestyle is changed. The early-day Salvation Army was justly proud of its 'trophies of grace'. These were people who had been enslaved by sin, and for whom salvation meant a total, radical transformation of their lives. People who were well known for a Godless way of life, changed completely, to the amazement of family, friends and the local community. For many of us the change is not so dramatic, but nevertheless a process is commenced which over the passage of time permeates and changes the way that we live.

When we become Christians there are some things we know and some things which remain unknown. As a consequence, hope affects many of the choices we make and how we live.

One of the things we become aware of when we come to faith is that we are children of God. This is the promise given in the beginning of John's Gospel. 'Yet to all who received him, to those who believed in his name, he gave the right to become children of God – children born not of natural descent, nor of human decision or a husband's will, but born of God (John 1:12, 13).

The same truth is expressed by Paul. 'For all who are led by the Spirit of God are children of God. So you have not received a spirit that makes you fearful slaves. Instead, you received God's Spirit when he adopted you as his own children. Now we call him,

"Abba, Father." For his Spirit joins with our spirit to affirm that we are God's children' (Romans 8:14–16 *NLT*).

Being a child of God not only brings us into a new relationship with God, but also with all who belong to the family of God. That is why Jesus died on the Cross, to bring together all the children of God scattered around the world. 'Jesus would die for the Jewish nation, and not only for that nation but also for the scattered children of God, to bring them together and make them one' (John 11:51, 52).

I can recall a period when I was the leader of a short-term project and had to form a secretariat to manage the workload. Although it was based at The Salvation Army's headquarters in Oslo, not every member was a Salvationist. After a while, one of the non-Salvationists commented to me that she noticed a difference in the relationships among Salvationists, as compared to the other employees. I could only reply that Salvationists were 'family', and that explained our relationship.

Like any other family, we do not necessarily like every member to the same degree, but we do belong just the same. The employee had noticed something, but could not easily pinpoint what it was. This family relationship exists between all believers, brought together by the love of Jesus and the grace of God.

More recently, my wife and I explained to one of our neighbours that we were going away on holiday, but while we were away there would be friends staying in our home. 'Who are they?' the neighbour asked. We don't know, we replied, they are members of a songster brigade (choir) visiting our corps (church). The neighbour was astonished that we could contemplate complete strangers living in our home while we were away. The only explanation we could give was that they would be like family, and it wouldn't be a problem. And it wasn't! It is wonderful the family network that is open to all who join the family of faith. This is one of the fruits of knowing we are God's children.

Another wonderful thing about being children of God is that we become heirs of the Kingdom. When we belong to Christ, we are the true children of Abraham. We are his heirs, and God's promise to Abraham belongs to us as Paul makes clear in Galatians 3:29.

During a difficult time in Scotland's history, a young Christian girl was on her way to a house meeting, which was forbidden at that time. She was stopped by soldiers who demanded to know where she was going and why. Not wanting to lie, she was suddenly inspired to give the following explanation. 'My brother has died,' she said, 'and the family is gathering to find out what we have inherited.' She was allowed to proceed, but the girl's answer was so profound. That is what happens when believers come together. It is like a family gathering. Jesus has died to bring us together, and we have become heirs with him to all the riches of the Kingdom.

This much we know, but what we do not know is what will become of us. It is true that Paul waxed eloquent over what we could expect as children of God. And we believers also groan, even though we have the Holy Spirit within us as a foretaste of future glory, for we long for our bodies to be released from sin and suffering. We, too, wait with eager hope for the day when God will give us our full rights as his adopted children, including the new bodies he has promised us (Romans 8:23; 1 Corinthians 15:44). However, what this will mean in detail is hidden from us, as again Paul reminds us when he quotes from Isaiah 64:4: 'For since the world began, no ear has heard, and no eye has seen a God like you, who works for those who wait for him!' (*NLT*; see also 1 Corinthians 2:9). All we can say is that there is a glorious future for all God's children. Of this we are sure, but we have to wait in hope for it to be revealed.

Does this mean that all that is required of us is to sit down and wait? No! Sometimes it does appear that contradictions occur in the Bible. For example: do we have to search for Jesus, as a collector searches for precious pearls? Or does Christ search for us like a shepherd searches for lost sheep? Do we, like Joshua, choose who we will serve (Joshua 24:15), or is it more correct to say that Christ has chosen us and not we him – 'You did not choose me, but I chose you' (John 15:16)?

There is no contradiction here but two sides of the same coin. His Spirit causes us to search for him, while Jesus stands at the door of our hearts and knocks. No one enters the Kingdom of God without making a conscious decision. Christ can seek entrance but we must let him in. The same applies to living in hope. Does it matter how we live? We cannot earn God's salvation. Only God can change us.

That brings us to this statement, which can be difficult to understand. 'Everyone who has this hope in him purifies himself, just as he is pure' (1 John 3:3).

John has more to say about this in his first letter; 'And as we live in God, our love grows more perfect. So we will not be afraid on the Day of Judgment, but we can face him with confidence because we live like Jesus here in this world' (1 John 4:17, *NLT*).

Christ calls us to a life with him, but we must rise up and follow him as did his first disciples. The keyword here is discipline. 'If anyone loves me, he will obey my teaching' (John 14:23). It is true to say that we are greatly influenced by what we see. Therefore if we look forward with hope to the future it will greatly affect the way we live today. We want to live like Jesus in the world, because one day we will see him face to face, and we want to be like him. Therefore as Christians we discipline ourselves.

'Don't you realise that in a race everyone runs, but only one person gets the prize? So run to win! All athletes are disciplined in their training. They do it to win a prize that will fade away, but we do it for an eternal prize' (1 Corinthians 9:24, 25, *NLT*).

In verse 27 (*NLT*) Paul says: 'I discipline my body like an athlete, training it to do what it should. Otherwise, I fear that after preaching to others I myself might be disqualified.' Discipline in the Christian life means not only avoiding evil and destructive things; it also means giving up things that are good in themselves for the greater good.

A young surgeon loved playing tennis. One day he noticed that the strenuous game was affecting his hands and hindering him in carrying out sensitive surgery. So he gave up playing tennis. There is nothing wrong with playing tennis, but for the greater cause the young surgeon had to lay it aside because it would hinder him in achieving his goal.

Our discipleship will almost certainly involve that kind of sacrifice. Peter and John gave up their fishing boats to become fishers of men. Peter once declared to Jesus, 'We've given up everything to follow you' (Mark 10:28, *NLT*). Discipline, therefore, does not just consist of departing from sin, it means putting aside other things as well. Immediately following the 'faith' chapter, Hebrews chapter 12 (*NLT*) begins with these words: 'Therefore, since we are surrounded by such a huge crowd of witnesses to the life of faith, let us strip off every weight that slows us down, especially the sin that so easily trips us up. And let us run with endurance the race God has set before us.'

Our hope for the future involves a life of preparation today, which affects the choices we make, and the lifestyle we live. But can we change? Is that a realistic hope? That question is considered in the next chapter.

CHANGE OR BE CHANGED.

'We could not save ourselves and we cannot hope to make ourselves holy, worthy to enter the presence of God.'

Chapter 11

Change or be changed

LIBERACE and Tessie O'shea were dancing together once on a TV show. Liberace exclaimed, 'I could dance like this forever!' Tessie responded: 'Don't you want to improve?'

It's a good question. Do we want to improve? Can we improve? Is there any hope of that happening? Not everyone wants to improve. They are quite happy and content as they are. They neither see the need, nor feel the desire, to improve in any capacity. Even though life is not necessarily good, some people are happy to remain as they are. When Jesus met a paralysed man at the Pool of Bethesda he asked, 'Do you want to get well?' (John 5:6). When he met the blind man at Jericho he asked, 'What do you want me to do for you?' (Mark 10:51).

Have you heard the light bulb-changing joke? How many psychiatrists does it take to change a light bulb? One! But the light bulb must want to be changed. It seems this principle was true for those Jesus helped. He was the one who could meet people's need, but it was important that they wanted to change. The trouble is that many people do not arrive at this point until they reach rock bottom.

It is not only the blind and the lame who need to change. We all need to, but many who are otherwise quite comfortable do not particularly want to change – like the selfish farmer in Luke 12:19 who said to himself, 'You have plenty of good things laid up for many years. Take life easy; eat, drink and be merry.' Why move out of the comfort zone?

'A man with leprosy came to Jesus and begged him on his knees, "If you are willing, you can make me clean"' (Mark 1:40). That man had already come far before he met Jesus. He wanted to change, and Jesus did not hesitate to answer his prayer.

The question remains however. Can we change if we want to? Does the situation described in Jeremiah 13:23 haunt us? 'Can the Ethiopian change his skin or the leopard its spots? Neither can you do good who are accustomed to doing evil'. Left to our own resources this condition is sadly true. Like trying to lift ourselves by our own hair, we try but it is impossible. Is there, then, hope for us, even though we want to change?

One day, after being astonished by his teaching, the disciples asked Jesus: '"Who then can be saved?" Jesus looked at them and said, "With man this is impossible, but with God all things are possible"' (Matthew 19:25b, 26).

It is one thing to heal physical disabilities, but something altogether different to heal and change the inner spiritual life, with its problems and disabilities. Jeremiah's question may not seem to provide much hope, but Ezekiel echoed God's word that there is hope for all of us: 'I will give them an undivided heart and put a new spirit in them; I will remove from them their heart of stone and give them a heart of flesh' (Ezekiel 11:19).

Jeremiah 31:33,34 says: '"This is the covenant I will make with the house of Israel after that time," declares the Lord. "I will put my law in their minds and write it on their hearts. I will be their God, and they will be my people. No longer will a man teach his neighbour, or a man his brother, saying, 'Know the Lord,' because they will all know me, from the least of them to the greatest," declares the Lord. "For I will forgive their wickedness and will remember their sins no more"'.

The work of salvation not only removes from us the guilt and power of sin, but it includes transforming us into a holy people. We could not save ourselves and we cannot hope to make ourselves holy, worthy to enter the presence of God.

When Isaiah confessed his sinful state in the Temple (Isaiah 6:5), he did not make himself clean. An angel touched his lips and he was purified. When Jesus called his disciples, he did not say follow me and you will be like me. He said '"Follow me and I will *make you* ... ."' (Mark 1:17). Christ, through his Spirit, makes us holy and our holiness reflects the glory of God, not our own achievements.

If this is Christ's work does it mean there is nothing we can do? No, not at all! We are called to follow him. This will be a life-changing process. We are called, chosen, to bear fruit. This will be our joy, but the glory will be his.

This is the hope that God provides for each one of us. In vain we try to improve ourselves spiritually, but the promise is there that God can and will create in us something new so that we are changed. This is our hope!

In 1 John 3:2 we read: 'Dear friends, now we are children of God, and what we will be has not yet been made known. But we know that when he appears, we shall be like him, for we shall see him as he is.' This is a work that begins when the regeneration power of the Holy Spirit is allowed into our lives.

John Gowans has said it so well:

> *To be like Jesus!*
> *This hope possesses me,*
> *In every thought and deed,*
> *This is my aim, my creed;*
> *To be like Jesus!*
> *This hope possesses me,*
> *His Spirit helping me,*
> *Like him I'll be.*

> (*SASB* chorus 107)

What a hope!

HOPE AND PERSECUTION.

'The truth is that Jesus wants us to remain
full of hope in the darkest hour.'

Chapter 12
Hope and persecution

MATTHEW 5:11–13 reads: 'Blessed are you when people insult you, persecute you and falsely say all kinds of evil against you because of me. Rejoice and be glad, because great is your reward in Heaven, for in the same way they persecuted the prophets who were before you.'

There are numerous references in the Gospels to Jesus and faith, and even more to Jesus and love, but Jesus is never recorded using the word hope, and when hope is mentioned at all it is usually in a negative context. Of the Jews it was said, 'They *hoped* to catch Jesus in something he said' (Luke 20:20). And Luke records, referring to Herod, 'From what he had heard about him, he *hoped* to see him perform some miracle' (23:8). Even the reference to the disciples on the Emmaus road was not very positive: 'We had hoped that he was the one who was going to redeem Israel' (Luke 24:21).

What can we deduce from this? Does it mean Jesus did not rate the quality of hope very highly?

Not at all! Although Jesus is not recorded as using the word hope, he implies its quality and importance repeatedly, and goes to great lengths to assure his disciples of the hope that is theirs. For example, just before his arrest and crucifixion Jesus said: 'Now is your time of grief, but I will see you again and you will rejoice, and no one will take away your joy' (John 16:22). Obviously Jesus was trying to prepare them for the worst, but at the same time he wanted to confirm that there was hope. He knew how important that was.

The opening verses of Matthew 5, often referred to as the Beatitudes, are filled with hope: verse 4 – those who mourn will be comforted; verse 5 – the meek will inherit the earth; verse 6 – those who hunger and thirst for righteousness will be filled; verse 7 – the merciful will be shown mercy; verse 8 – the pure in heart will see God; and it can all be summed up in verse 12 – rejoice and be glad because great is your reward in Heaven. This isn't just hoping for the best, this is the hope which Christ gives all believers and is the true source of joy and happiness.

Peter, on the day of Pentecost, preaching the first Christian sermon, confirmed this by quoting a psalm of David: 'Therefore my heart is glad and my tongue rejoices; my body also will live in hope' (Acts 2:26).

Many people are willing to offer thanksgiving and praise to God when life is good, and they see evidence of blessing and prosperity surrounding their lives. The truth is that Jesus wants us to remain full of hope in the darkest hour. He gave hope to the disciples by telling them before grief and tragedy struck that these things would pass, and they would eventually experience a joy that no one could take from them.

Paul and Silas certainly learnt this lesson well when in the innermost cell of the prison at Philippi. Their backs smarting from a whipping received earlier in the day, and shackled with heavy chains, unable to sleep, they had no guarantee that they would survive the experience which so unjustly had been thrust upon them by their enemies. Even so, in the dark, cold dungeon of the prison they resorted to singing songs of praise in the middle of the night. The psalmist says weeping may remain for a night, but rejoicing comes in the morning. There certainly was rejoicing in the morning in the home of the Philippian jail keeper.

It is believed that all the disciples of Jesus met with violent deaths, becoming martyrs, except for Judas, who died at his own hand and possibly John who died a natural death. However, Jesus knew that not only the disciples, but everyone who would follow in their footsteps must be prepared to take up their cross. Persecution, grief and martyrdom have always been evident in the life of the Church.

Since the death of Jesus Christ 2,000 years ago, it is estimated that 43 million Christians have become martyrs. More than half of these have been martyred in the past 100 years. Today it is estimated that some 200 million Christians around the world experience persecution because of their faith, and of this number 60 per cent are children. Every day more than 300 are killed for their faith in Jesus Christ. These figures are likely to increase in the future, rather than decrease.

The Salvation Army, working in nearly 120 countries, is not exempt from persecution. Reports of such from various parts of the world fill our hearts with sadness, yet Christ declares that people caught up in such situations should not despair, but rejoice. This is incredible. How can this be expected? Yet the fact is that we have a hope in Christ that nothing can destroy.

Paul says, quoting psalm 44:22, 'For your sake we face death all day long; we are considered as sheep to be slaughtered' then adds, 'No, in all these things we are more than conquerors through him who loved us. For I am convinced that neither death nor life, neither angels nor demons, neither the present nor the future, nor any powers, neither height nor depth, nor anything else in all creation, will be able to separate us from the love of God that is in Christ Jesus our Lord' (Romans 8:36-39).

This is the tremendous truth that Jesus has given us. He doesn't say in the face of these things, 'Don't despair!' Incredibly he says, 'Rejoice and be glad!' Christians are not called to be survivors, but conquerors through the victory Christ won by his death and resurrection. If on Easter Sunday we rejoice over a naked cross, an empty tomb and a risen Saviour, we should also rejoice when we are called upon to make a similar sacrifice.

It may be that we as Christians may not have to face persecution on such a scale as having to face martyrdom, but it does mean possessing the willingness, discipline and dedication to follow Christ whatever the cost. When we are confronted by setbacks because of our faith, let us not forget to rejoice because of the hope we have.

Even in the face of death we can rejoice: 'Your dead will live; their bodies will rise. You who dwell in the dust, wake up and shout for joy. Your dew is like the dew of the morning; the earth will give birth to her dead' (Isaiah 26:19).

Remember, everything will be OK at the end. If it's not OK, it's not the end!

HOPE IS IN EVERYTHING.

"The element of hope is in the details. We know the central things, but not all the details."

Chapter 13

Hope is in everything

'IF you lose hope, somehow you lose the vitality that keeps life moving, you lose that courage to be, that quality that helps you go on in spite of it all. And so today I still have a dream' (Martin Luther King).

There is no doubt about it, if you lose hope you lose something that is essential to life. Hope can be likened to a belief that events and circumstances will lead to something positive. Hope can be likened to a feeling that events will turn out for the best. 'The pessimist sees difficulty in every opportunity. The optimist sees the opportunity in every difficulty,' said Winston Churchill. Hope is all this and more. For the Christian it is a virtue together with faith and love. It is an awareness of spiritual truth, and therefore is distinct from positive thinking and physical emotion. Therefore we rejoice in the hope of the glory of God (Romans 5:2).

As Christians our life is permeated with hope. We can experience hope that can sustain us and others in a crisis, like Paul when caught up in a frightening storm on the way to Rome. In the middle of the storm he was a calming influence when he said to the ship's company, 'But now I urge you to keep up your courage, because not one of you will be lost; only the ship will be destroyed' (Acts 27:22). We can experience hope against hope, when we still hope even when there is no rational ground to justify hope, like Abraham: 'Against all hope, Abraham in hope believed and so became the father of many nations' (Romans 4:18).

Then there is the hope which affects the way we live: 'Everyone who has this hope in him purifies himself, just as he is pure'

(1 John 3:3). Basically, the hope of the Christian is rooted in the Resurrection of Jesus Christ. Because Jesus rose from the dead we have the sure and certain hope that we will too. 'Praise be to the God and Father of our Lord Jesus Christ! In his great mercy he has given us new birth into a living hope through the resurrection of Jesus Christ from the dead' (1 Peter 1:3).

The Christian hope is not something we do, it is something we have. The Christian does not say I am hoping for the best, he says with Paul: 'We know that in all things God works for the good of those who love him, who have been called according to his purpose' (Romans 8:28).

Paul here speaks of hope as knowing. By this Paul means that, because hope is something we have and not something we do, we are not hoping, we know. The element of hope therefore is in the details. We know the central things, but not all the details. We know that Christ rose from the dead, we don't know how. We know he will return one day in glorious triumph, we don't know when. We know there will be a new earth and a new Heaven, but it is beyond our wildest imagination to envisage what that will involve. We know that one day we will have a glorified body, but what form it will take is a mystery.

'Our citizenship is in Heaven. And we eagerly await a Saviour from there, the Lord Jesus Christ, who, by the power that enables him to bring everything under his control, will transform our lowly bodies so that they will be like his glorious body' (Philippians 3:20–22).

At the beginning of his term as General of The Salvation Army, John Gowans presented a definition of the Army's mission which has often been quoted since. He said that the purpose of the Army is threefold: to save sinners, grow saints and serve suffering humanity. In this concise summary the Army's purpose has been expressed in a nutshell. However, it could be expressed even more briefly as follows: the Army's purpose is hope, hope, hope!

There is the hope of salvation. We are intent on bringing hope to people. When we bring the message of salvation to people we are at the same time giving them the means of receiving hope. We have been called to make known the glorious riches of this mystery, which is Christ in you, the hope of glory. If we were to bring hope in Christ only for this life we would be the object of pity for all men. But we are called upon to proclaim to all people of every clime that there is eternal life and hope to be found in Christ. Not for the years of time alone, but for eternity.

Then there is the hope of a holy life. When Jesus rose from the dead, he had a glorified body, but his former body was not left to rot in the grave. It is an essential part of the Easter story, and of the gospel we proclaim, that the grave was empty. His new body took the elements from his earthly body and transformed them. This should have the effect of showing us that in being spiritual beings we are not to neglect our physical bodies. What we are in this life will be part of what we are to become; therefore, because of this hope, the hope that we will one day be like him, we do not neglect our bodies.

We do not say: one day we will leave this body behind, so it is not important what we do with it. We should rather say: I will glorify God in my body, it shall be his temple. It is this hope that motivates our holiness, a holiness that is practical, that also considers the physical consequences of our living, that our whole being might glorify God. This is why the Salvationist seeks a lifestyle that does just that – glorifies God in our bodies.

We do not become so Heavenly-minded that we forget completely the things of this world which affect how we live and what we are. The concept of holiness loses its motivation if there is no hope. We are possessed of a hope, and therefore we seek, through God's grace, to live holy lives

Finally, there is the concept of suffering humanity. This is so vast as to be almost impossible for us to comprehend. Yet we are called to serve those who are in need and are suffering. By our ministry, whether we are seeking out people in the gutter, sitting beside a hospital bed, visiting those in prison, or bringing food, drink and clothing to people overtaken by a catastrophe, the object is the same. We want to show the love of God, and we want to bring hope where there does not seem to be any.

In 1 Corinthians 13, Paul says that when he became a man he put away childish things. Put another way, he implies that he was no longer taken up with the things that occupied him when he was a child. He also adds that three things remain: faith, hope and love. The greatest of these is love. Faith is important, but let us not forget hope. It has been placed between the other two, and can be said to link them together.

Memento mori is a Latin phrase that may be translated 'Remember you are mortal'. In ancient Rome, the phrase is said to have been used on the occasions when a Roman general was parading through the streets of Rome during a victory celebration known as a triumph. Standing behind the victorious general was a slave who had the task of reminding the general that, though he was on a peak today, tomorrow was another day. The servant did this by telling the general that he should remember that he was mortal: *Memento mori*. It may be good if we remind ourselves of that truth, but let us temper it with another Latin word: *resurgam* – 'I will arise'. Receiving hope, living in hope and bringing hope to others is our mission. This is our hope and this is our joy.

WE WILL SEE JESUS.

'The number one place went to Jesus Christ!'

Chapter 14

We will see Jesus

A POLL was held in the UK in which 3,000 people were asked which dead person they would most love to meet. William Shakespeare came third, physicist Albert Einstein fourth and Hollywood legend Marilyn Monroe fifth. Leonardo da Vinci – best known for painting the Mona Lisa – took sixth place and Elvis Presley, king of rock and roll, came seventh. However the top two places are surprising. In second place came Princess Diana, who was killed in a car crash in 1997, and the number one place went to Jesus Christ!

What can we say in the light of this poll? First, on a technical point, Jesus should have been disqualified from the list. The poll made only one condition. The person nominated had to be dead. Jesus is alive. He is out of this world, but he is not dead.

Second, all those who would like to meet Jesus will get their wish fulfilled. The message of the Bible is quite clear on this point. Jesus will one day return to this world: 'Look, he is coming with the clouds, and every eye will see him, even those who pierced him' (Revelation 1:7).

Jesus has not always been the most popular person. On one occasion everyone present cried out for him to be crucified. These, too, will see Jesus. Once some Greeks approached Philip and said, 'We would see Jesus', and the good news is that all who make the same prayer will be answered. That may be surprising news to some, but for countless others it is their hope and source of joy and inspiration.

NOTHING
IS IN VAIN.

'We have a glorious hope, and nothing we do for
the Lord in this life is in vain.'

Chapter 15

Nothing is in vain

THERE seem to be two dominant conflicting views regarding the future. One typical view shared by the world of advertising and politicians is basically optimistic. There is a brave new and better world just around the corner. There is always an improved, greener and cheaper product being announced to consumers. Some producers describe themselves as leading the way, without describing in detail where they are leading to. Politicians, on the other hand, proclaim an optimistic future if and when they come to power. Some may confess that things will get worse before they get better, but they will get better. They proclaim change; change for the better.

On the other hand, and in marked contrast, is the essentially pessimistic view of the scientific community. This view encompasses a list of catastrophes which sooner or later will wreak havoc on a global scale. Such things as climate change, nuclear war, giant meteors, monstrous volcanoes, earthquakes, population explosion with accompanying disasters such as war, famine, pandemic diseases, even alien invasions from outer space. And if we manage to survive all these threats and dangers, finally the sun will expand and burn the earth to a cinder. The scientist no longer wonders what life will be like in the future. He wonders if there will be life in the future. What real hope is there then without God? In a word, looked at from this point of view, there is no hope.

What, then, is the Christian hope seen in this light? How should it affect us? Again there are two views.

One view is that we are living in the last days. God is going to fulfil prophecy. He will manifest himself in a new way, and roll up creation like an old cloth. The faithful will be taken to Heaven, and the rest doomed to be cast into the everlasting fire. This viewpoint produces the attitude of *laissez-faire*. There is nothing to be done, just sit back and wait. Like a car about to be taken to the breakers, they see no point in oiling the motor, or polishing the bodywork. Doing anything to improve the world is simply a waste of time.

The error here is that such people consider creation to be of no lasting importance, only the 'spiritual' matters. They see no future for creation and no point in being concerned with this world.

There is another view. When God created the world he declared that it was good. Mankind was given the responsibility of tending it: 'Rule over the fish of the sea and the birds of the air and over every living creature that moves on the ground' (Genesis 1:28).

In the following chapter we read: 'The Lord God took the man and put him in the Garden of Eden to work it and take care of it' (v. 15). It is clear that we have a responsibility for the stewardship of this created world and this responsibility is still with us. We must not say that the world is coming to an end and therefore it does not matter if we pollute the environment and cause the extinction of other living creatures by our greed and indifference. We must avoid being so spiritually-minded that we are of no earthly good.

Martin Luther was once asked what he would do if the world would end tomorrow. He answered, 'I would plant a tree today.' The world may well end tomorrow, and we must be prepared for that, but we must live as though it will continue forever. This means investing in the future, not giving up.

Paul came with this exhortation in 1 Corinthians 15:58: 'Therefore, my dear brothers, stand firm. Let nothing move you. Always give yourselves fully to the work of the Lord, because you know that your labour in the Lord is not in vain.' This is the hope that must be our inspiration; nothing we do for the Lord is in vain.

Again Paul reminds us in Galatians 6:9: 'Let us not become weary in doing good, for at the proper time we will reap a harvest if we do not give up.' Christ didn't give up, even praying for those around him while on the way to the Cross. By his grace we must not give up, but continue to care for this world.

After his Resurrection, Christ's new, resurrected body could do things that his former body could not do, yet it was based on the former. His earthly body did not lie in the grave to rot, it was resurrected into something more glorious. Because of our hope for the future, a hope which says that what we are and do in this life will influence the world to come and our place in it, we must not neglect the world in which we dwell, nor our body, which is the temple of the living God.

As we read in Philippians 3:21, Jesus will transform our lowly bodies so that they will be like his glorious body. The word transform implies that our body will not be cast away and replaced by a new one. Transform means that our essential identity, contained in our earthly bodies, will be present in the resurrected body.

A question which might possibly arise from this last statement is: 'What about those who have been cremated, or for whom there is no grave?' This is no problem for our Creator. During our lifetime our body materials constantly change. Not just hair or fingernails, but every atom of our body is completely changed every seven years or so. However our personality, thoughts and memories continue.

I believe it was C. S. Lewis who used the illustration of a waterfall, in which the water is constantly changing, but the form remains the same. So with us; what our bodies physically consist of is subject to constant change, but the real self continues and matures. Peter speaks of a new Heaven and a new earth, and draws the conclusion that our hope should affect the way we live today. 'But in keeping with his promise we are looking forward to a new Heaven and a new earth, the home of righteousness. So then, dear friends, since you are looking forward to this, make every effort to be found spotless, blameless and at peace with him' (2 Peter 3:13, 14).

We have a glorious hope, and nothing we do for the Lord in this life is in vain.

HOPE AT THE END!

'Perhaps of all living creatures we are unique
in one respect, we know that we will die.
It is surely the one certainty in life.'

Chapter 16

Hope at the end

I REMEMBER having a conversation with an acquaintance of mine who came from Sri Lanka. He was a nominal Buddhist and mentioned to me one day that he was celebrating their New Year. 'What year are you now beginning?' I asked. Remembering that the Islamic year is about 580 years behind the Christian (Gregorian) calendar, I wondered, in my ignorance, whether the Buddhist calendar was a few thousand years ahead. He gave me a blank look and replied, 'I don't know!'

This surprised me initially, but I have since reflected on it, and it appears that ancient oriental cultures have a totally different relationship from the West to the passing of time. Even the start of the Buddhist New Year varies from country to country. In Sri Lanka and Cambodia it starts on the first full moon in January; in Thailand, in April. Then again, China has a 12-year cycle named after animals: rat, ox, tiger, hare, dragon, snake, horse, sheep, monkey, rooster, dog, pig. Although Japan now uses the Gregorian calendar, it still numbers its years after the reigning monarch, something like the system in ancient Jewish history. The year 2000, for example, which happened to be the 12th year of the reign of the current emperor, whose posthumous name will be Heisei, was called Heisei 12.

All this stands in contrast to the calendar we in the West are familiar with, which takes as its reference point the birth of Christ. For us, time does not go in an eternal circle but is lineal, having a beginning and consequently an end. This situation therefore begs the question, what happens when we reach the end of our earthly lives? What is our hope when time meets its consummation at the end of days?

Perhaps of all living creatures we are unique in one respect, we know that we will die. It is surely the one certainty in life. We may not dwell on the thought, and may even try to avoid it, but it is there, and sooner or later we will have to come to terms with it.

There are endless jokes on the subject of life after death, and the cartoons on the subject are also without number. Will we really sit about on clouds all day, playing harps, equipped with wings and a halo? It is difficult to say where these images and stories come from, but it isn't the teaching of the Bible. True there is a certain amount of symbolism in the Bible. The Pearly Gates can refer to the fact that pearls are the only jewels produced by pain, and it was at enormous cost and pain that the entrance into Heaven was obtained. Then there are the streets paved with gold, reminding us that the most precious metal here on earth is treated as asphalt by Heaven's standards. For many people getting saved means going to Heaven when you die, however the Bible has little to say about Heaven and how to get there. If we study the messages of the apostles, they did not have much to say about going to Heaven, it was more a case of Heaven coming to us.

There is a lot of speculation regarding what happens when we die, and it is not my intention to add to that. I therefore want to keep to the concept of hope, and what we know. Of course we do not know all the details about what the future contains for us, but there are definite signposts pointing in that direction that can give confidence to our hope. Here are some of the things we know.

The first thing we can say is that Jesus was at the start of things and he will be at the finish. In Revelation we read: 'I am the Alpha and the Omega, the First and the Last, the Beginning and the End' (1:8; 21:6; 22:13). Jesus was present at creation's morn, as the opening verses of John's Gospel declare: 'In the beginning was the Word, and the Word was with God, and the Word was God. He was with God in the beginning. Through him all things were made; without him nothing was made that has been made.' It was he who took the initiative at the start of our discipleship: 'You did not choose me, but I chose you and appointed you to go and bear fruit – fruit that will last' (John 15:16).

The psalmist speaks of the omnipresence of God, and states: 'You hem me in – behind and before; you have laid your hand upon me' (Psalm 139:5). Jesus is always in the eternal now: '"I tell you the truth," Jesus answered, "before Abraham was born, I am!"' (John 8:58). The writer of Hebrews expressed in praise: 'Jesus Christ is the same yesterday and today and forever' (Hebrews 13:8). Therefore the first definite thing we can say about the end of our lives, and the end of time, is that the same Jesus who was at the start of things, and who has been the unseen presence in our lives, will be there!

We know too that there will be a new Heaven and a new earth. Peter says: 'We are looking forward to a new Heaven and a new earth, the home of righteousness' (2 Peter 3:13). It will be a new and therefore transformed earth. Perhaps then the prayer of our Lord will be answered: 'Thy will be done on earth as it is in Heaven.'

That prayer is also the cause for hope. It is the hope and desire of Jesus that God's will be done, and therefore with confidence we can look forward to the day when that will be realised. Paul also expresses the truth in Romans 8:19–25 that our hope in Christ also encompasses creation. 'The creation waits in eager expectation for the sons of God to be revealed. For the creation was subjected to frustration, not by its own choice, but by the will of the one who subjected it, in hope that the creation itself will be liberated from its bondage to decay and brought into the glorious freedom of the children of God. We know that the whole creation has been groaning as in the pains of childbirth right up to the present time. Not only so, but we ourselves, who have the firstfruits of the Spirit, groan inwardly as we wait eagerly for our adoption as sons, the redemption of our bodies. For in this hope we were saved. But hope that is seen is no hope at all. Who hopes for what he already has? But if we hope for what we do not yet have, we wait for it patiently.'

Some people are of the opinion that we will leave this world and fly off to Heaven, and refer to 1 Thessalonians 4:16–18: 'For the Lord himself will come down from Heaven, with a loud command, with the voice of the archangel and with the trumpet call of God, and the dead in Christ will rise first. After that, we who are still alive and are left will be caught up together with them in the clouds to meet the Lord in the air. And so we will be with the Lord forever. Therefore encourage each other with these words.'

Yet to assume from this that we will all leave this earth is to misunderstand the situation. The words 'together we will be caught up in the air to meet the Lord, and so be with him forever' do not mean we will all leave this world. Jesus will not be leaving, he will be arriving, as the angels proclaimed on the day of his Ascension: 'Why do you stand here looking into the sky? This same Jesus, who has been taken from you into Heaven, will come back in the same way you have seen him go into Heaven' (Acts 1:11). The custom was then, as now, that whenever an important head of state made an arrival, people went out to meet him and accompany him into the city. That is what the people did on Palm Sunday. 'They took palm branches and went out to meet him, shouting, 'Hosanna! Blessed is he who comes in the name of the Lord! Blessed is the King of Israel!' (John 12:13). This is the scene Paul describes in 1 Thessalonians. The people were meeting Jesus to escort him in, never again to be parted.

Another truth is that there will be the resurrection of the dead, after the example given to us by Jesus. Daniel 12:2: 'Multitudes who sleep in the dust of the earth will awake: some to everlasting life, others to shame and everlasting contempt.'

Isaiah also foresees it: 'But your dead will live; their bodies will rise. You who dwell in the dust, wake up and shout for joy. Your dew is like the dew of the morning; the earth will give birth to her dead' (Isaiah 26:19).

We do not know when all this will happen. There has been much discussion on the subject, but it is clear from Scripture that it has not taken place yet. In the sixth chapter of John, Jesus repeatedly refers to raising people up on the last day. Martha also refers to it after the death of Lazarus: 'I know he will rise again in the resurrection at the last day' (John 11:24). It has been suggested that in the meantime the dead are resting in Paradise. This can be argued from the fact that Jesus promised the dying thief that he would that same day be with Jesus in Paradise.

Obviously this is something other than resurrection. Even Jesus was not resurrected on Good Friday. As I have already said, we do not know everything, but we do have signposts pointing the way, and we will not truly know everything until we arrive at our destination.

There will be a final judgment. You might think this sounds negative and not much of a hope, but judgment here means righting the wrongs and injustices of history. Mary referred to this in the Magnificat: 'His mercy extends to those who fear him, from generation to generation. He has performed mighty deeds with his arm; he has scattered those who are proud in their inmost thoughts. He has brought down rulers from their thrones but has lifted up the humble. He has filled the hungry with good things but has sent the rich away empty' (Luke 1:50–53).

Micah puts it like this: 'He will judge between many peoples and will settle disputes for strong nations far and wide. They will beat their swords into ploughshares and their spears into pruning hooks. Nation will not take up sword against nation, nor will they train for war anymore' (Micah 4:3).

Everyone will see Jesus for who he is: 'Therefore God exalted him to the highest place and gave him the name that is above every name, that at the name of Jesus every knee should bow, in Heaven and on earth and under the earth, and every tongue confess that Jesus Christ is Lord, to the glory of God the Father' (Philippians 2:9–11).

We will be rewarded: 'Behold, I am coming soon! My reward is with me, and I will give to everyone according to what he has done' (Revelation 22:12). Many do not like the sound of being rewarded, considering that we are saved by grace through faith and not by works, but there are several references to rewards in the New Testament. Jesus mentioned them in his teaching. He taught: 'Love your enemies, do good to them, and lend to them without expecting to get anything back. Then your reward will be great' (Luke 6:35). In the parable of the talents we read: 'His master replied, "Well done, good and faithful servant! You have been faithful with a few things; I will put you in charge of many things. Come and share your master's happiness!"' (Matthew 25:23). However, we must not think of reward in terms of money. Jesus spoke of those who showed their diligence in faithfully tending to small matters being rewarded with even greater responsibility. This brings us to the next point.

We will have work to do, and we will relish doing it. We will not be lazing around on a cloud all day. Timothy speaks of us as reigning with Christ: 'If we endure, we will also reign with him' (2 Timothy 2:12). I have already quoted Jesus saying that faithfulness will result in us being put in charge of greater things, and thereby sharing Christ's happiness. This truth is also repeated in Luke 12: 42–44: 'The Lord answered, "Who then is the faithful and wise manager, whom the master puts in charge of his servants to give them their food allowance at the proper time? It will be good for that servant whom the master finds doing so when he returns. I tell you the truth, he will put him in charge of all his possessions."' The first Adam was entrusted to care and tend creation, and so there will be tasks awaiting us in the new Heaven and new earth.

There is another aspect of what we already know, and that is that we will know much more then than we can possibly know now. There are so many things that happen in this life that we cannot understand. Like the psalmist we cry: 'O Lord God Almighty, how long will your anger smoulder against the prayers of your people?' (Psalm 80:4). It is as though in this life we see the reverse side of a tapestry, with only hints of what is being created. The time will come when we shall see things from the other side and the whole picture is finally seen. Paul encourages us in 1 Corinthians 13:12 where he writes: 'Now we see but a poor reflection as in a mirror;

then we shall see face to face. Now I know in part; then I shall know fully, even as I am fully known.'

This chapter cannot be concluded without mentioning the things that will not be around at the end. 'There will be no more death or mourning or crying or pain, for the old order of things has passed away' (Revelation 21:4). There will be no more night. We will not need the light of a lamp or the light of the sun, for the Lord God will give us light. And there will be no end to our joy in the Lord. 'We have this hope as an anchor for the soul, firm and secure. It enters the inner sanctuary behind the curtain, where Jesus, who went before us, has entered on our behalf' (Hebrews 6:19,20).

I have not covered everything that could be said about life after death, but then neither does the 11th doctrine of The Salvation Army which simply states: 'We believe in the immortality of the soul; in the resurrection of the body; in the general judgment at the end of the world; in the eternal happiness of the righteous; and in the endless punishment of the wicked.' However, I have tried to emphasise the living hope that is the precious possession of all who believe, and tried to correct some misconceptions that appear to be prevalent amongst both Christians and non Christians. What a hope we have!

HOPE AND DEATH.

'Let us keep a sense of proportion regarding death.
It is an enemy, but it is a beaten foe.'

Chapter 17

Hope and death

DEATH is the only inescapable, unavoidable, sure thing. We are sentenced to die the day we're born. So why am I mentioning this in a book about hope? It is because we need to see death for what it is if we want to live life to the full. Ecclesiastes 7:2 puts it like this:' It is better to go to a house of mourning than to go to a house of feasting, for death is the destiny of every man; the living should take this to heart'.

I do not for a moment suggest that we become preoccupied with death. The 17th-century writer La Rochefoucauld wrote, 'Neither the sun nor death can be looked at with a steady eye'. Ian Fleming, author of the James Bond books, wrote, 'You only live twice. Once when you are born and once when you look death in the face'. Under certain conditions we can stare at the sun, and there are also times when we can and must consider death.

When I was a teenager, death had a fascination for me. Not a morbid one. I was a Salvation Army bandsman at the time, and our band often turned out to play at the funerals of soldiers of the corps. I had an understanding employer, and whenever I asked to be absent for a funeral I was given permission to leave work early. I felt that as we paid our last respects to these comrades, the circle of their lives was completed, and we were making the farewell from this life a worthy one. A few years later, as an officer, I felt it an honour to conduct the funerals of those who had reached the end of their lives. I always felt it to be a privilege.

While I had a feeling of satisfaction over funerals, it wasn't so easy dealing with people who were dying. What can one say to people in that situation? I remember visiting a woman in hospital who was terminally ill, and as I made my way to her ward I wondered what I would find. Imagine my surprise when I found her sitting up in bed greeting me with the words of Isaiah 12:2: 'Surely God is my salvation; I will trust and not be afraid'. She was radiant and full of joy. I visited her with the hope of bringing her some blessing, but it was I who was filled with blessing as I left the hospital that day.

'Blessed are the dead who die in the Lord' (Revelation 14:13) is a truth that I have witnessed, but this does not deny the fact that death is an enemy. It is an enemy when it claims the life of a young child before he or she has had a chance to grow up into a fulfilled life, leaving in its wake heartbroken parents and families tragically diminished. It is a sad mystery when death claims the life of a young parent, when the spouse and children stand by an open grave and question, 'Why?' Even when people bring death upon themselves by thoughtless living, we know God takes no delight in their death. 'As surely as I live, declares the Sovereign LORD, I take no pleasure in the death of the wicked' (Ezekiel 33:11). Whether young or old, rich or poor, death the reaper will remove us all from this life, unless the Lord returns before our time is up.

So having stared at death, and admitted its inevitability, what hope is there for us? First we must remember that if death is an enemy, God is stronger than his foes, and in the midst of death, we must remember that even death can be used by God in this life to fulfil his purposes. The death of Stephen, the first Christian martyr, made a great impression on Saul and opened the pathway to his conversion on the way to Damascus. Later Tertullian would coin the phrase, 'The blood of the martyrs is the seed of the Church.'

Then Jesus reminds us that death is not the worst thing that can happen to us: 'Do not be afraid of those who kill the body but cannot kill the soul' (Matthew 10:28). Let us keep a sense of proportion regarding death. It is an enemy, but it is a beaten foe.

Thirdly, we must not let the fear of death win over us. United States President Obama in his inauguration speech said: 'We have chosen hope over fear.' We must do the same, and diligently use the time we have, while we have the opportunity. Jesus said: 'As long as it is day, we must do the work of him who sent me. Night is coming, when no one can work' (John 9:4).

Paul said that he looked forward to the day when Christ concludes a total victory, including a victory over death: 'For he must reign until he has put all his enemies under his feet. The last enemy to be destroyed is death' (1 Corinthians 15:25,26). The entry of death into history is first recorded in the first book of the Bible, and in the last book of the Bible we can read of its end: 'He will wipe every tear from their eyes. There will be no more death' (Revelation 21:4).

When the perishable has been clothed with the imperishable, and the mortal with immortality, then the saying that is written will come true: 'Death has been swallowed up in victory' (1 Corinthians 15:54b). This is the hope we have that death is not the last word. Evil shall perish, and righteousness will reign. What a hope!

Epilogue

'SOME see things the way they are and ask, "Why?" I dream things that never were, and ask, "Why not?"' (George Bernard Shaw)

During the writing of this book about hope, numerous insights and revelations have come to me. What started out as a couple of articles has increasingly developed. It was as if every time I finished a chapter a new one presented itself, pleading to be written. Hope has taken on a new meaning for me.

For example, Jesus is never recorded as using the word hope, but by his life, teaching, death and resurrection he has given us hope. It has been my growing conviction that we are called not simply to proclaim God's love, but to show it. Our calling is not just to preach faith, but to exercise it so that by our words and our lives we give hope to others.

Soon after the recommencement of The Salvation Army's work in Russia I travelled with a truckload of humanitarian aid to St Petersburg. My driver was a farmer who took on jobs such as this one when extra help was needed. We had travelled from Norway, through Sweden and Finland. His farmer's eye had observed things that went unnoticed by me. He pointed out that in the western countries we had driven through, the fields were ploughed ready for the early spring harvest, and there were corn silos to be seen everywhere.

But in Russia, travelling through similar countryside, he hadn't seen one ploughed field nor a single silo. When we arrived at our destination I asked my host the reason for this. He reminded me that before communism had taken over, Russia had been the main exporter of grain to Europe. Now people on the land only grew enough for themselves. If they grew more, there were not the logistics in place to get their produce to market, and even if they tried, corruption and crime would destroy any hope they might have of improving their lot. So they had given up.

I thought to myself, where do you start to turn around a country like Russia? There is no easy answer to that question, but it will not be found in preaching about God's love. They will simply say, 'Don't talk to us about God's love, show us yours!' It will not be found in exhorting people to exercise faith. They will only seek the evidence of the faith our lives reveal. They need to be given hope. This is our calling, to spread love and share our faith in order to bring hope. That is what The Salvation Army is doing in Russia.

It is not only Russia that has problems; we can look at the whole world and ask why things are the way they are, with war, famine, sickness, financial crises, crime, family breakdown and corruption. Standing by and asking, 'Why?' will not help. As Christians we must be people of hope, revealing the love of God in selfless service, attempting the seemingly impossible through faith.

We need to be the kind of people who, through Jesus Christ, rejoice in the hope and the glory of God, and who kindle that hope in others – because we have hope … what a hope!